Surviving Wonderland

A Journey Beyond Control

Brittany Hart

Tehom Center Publishing is a 501(c)3 nonprofit publishing feminist and queer authors, with a commitment to elevate BIPOC writers. Its face and voice is Rev. Dr. Angela Yarber.

Paperback ISBN: 978-1-966655-58-9

Ebook ISBN: 978-1-966655-59-6

For Deborah Perkins,

I am forever indebted to your bravery in coming forward to tell your story. The awareness and healing reflected in the following pages would not exist otherwise. Thank you.

Contents

Prologue

No one is more surprised than me that this book exists. Like many religious cult or high-control group survivors, when you're in it, you never imagine disagreeing or (God forbid) challenging that community. Sadly, as too many statistics and stories now show, this has become an all too prevalent reality. There comes a time when the smoke fades and the mirrors shatter, obliterating everything we knew in its wake. My obliteration came slowly. We'll get to that. But first, let me take you back to the beginning. To a young girl who rushed hard and fast into something because she was just trying to love Jesus.

For most of my young adult life, I was known as "The IHOP Girl." And no, it wasn't because of an undying love for pancakes (although that's true, too). It was a reference to a Christian community called the International House of Prayer in Kansas City (IHOP-KC). IHOPKC was a ministry with a 24/7 worship and prayer room whose teachings centered around intimacy with God and preparing for the "end times."

I first encountered IHOPKC when I was sixteen. I attended their youth conference and had some genuinely beautiful experiences with God. This was coupled with an impassioned introduction to their theology and mission. Their founder, Mike Bickle, believed we were living in "the generation of the Lord's return" and that God was raising "the best of the best" to usher in Jesus' second coming through night and day prayer. As a new Christian fervently seeking a deeper relationship with God, I was sold. If a godly man, who also claimed to have countless supernatural encounters, said *this* was the thing to do, then it felt like a no-brainer. So I jumped on board without a second thought.

It soon became my whole personality. I watched the prayer room webstream for two hours, everyday after school. Every weekend I was listening to leaders preach about the end times. Instead of going to college, I joined one of their summer internships two weeks after my high school graduation. Like the young girl in the beloved children's story *Alice in Wonderland*, I was fascinated by Mike Bickle's erratic energy. He was the White Rabbit I followed, tumbling down into a Wonderland of religious frenzy.

Similar to the fictional Wonderland, IHOPKC was full of magical moments and baffling characters. Some of the best musicians and singers occupied the stage of their 24/7 prayer room, renowned theologians spoke at their school, and their conferences pulled in thousands. In the beginning, I couldn't get enough. I was deeply engrossed from afar and when I eventually moved there, it felt like home.

This changed in 2012 after completing a year of their ministry school. It'd be an understatement to say that this school was physically, mentally, and spiritually demanding. Every day, you'd be the recipient of their theological firehose, on top of having to spend at least 24 hours a week in the prayer room. You were encouraged to cover your expenses by raising financial support like an oversees missionary. But if you were like me and weren't able to raise enough, you had to work regardless of their impossible schedule. So I was regularly pulling fifteen hour days with little to no regard for the toll it was taking on my overall health.

The leadership wasn't entirely oblivious to how taxing this all was. On the contrary, we were told it was intentional. I once heard a leader say, "We know this schedule is tough. It's meant to break you." And then they used biblical stories to back that up.

Combine all of this with an overall feeling that you were never doing enough or that you weren't as dedicated as everyone else, and you've got a perfect recipe for a breakdown.

When my breaking happened, I had to distance myself from all their teachings and couldn't even step foot in the prayer room. I didn't have the language for it then, but it's clear now that I was experiencing post-traumatic stress symptoms.

Even though I was starting to see some of their unhealthy patterns, if you'd asked me how I felt about them then, I would have said, "That isn't really for me anymore but I still have the utmost respect for Mike Bickle and the leaders." I had no idea that those feelings would shatter in October 2023.

I'll never forget sitting on my couch, enjoying a casual Friday night, when my friend texted me, "Have you heard about Mike Bickle?" I had no idea what she was talking about, but I was completely dumbfounded when she shared the allegations of sexual abuse that came out against him.

Mike was the absolute last man on the planet that I *ever* imagined doing something like this. I didn't know him personally, but from afar, he was the most joyful and godly man I knew of. He regularly taught about intimacy with Jesus and the importance of a prayer life. He smiled at you and gave you high-fives in the prayer room. He lived a seemingly humble and simple life. He seemed so great from the outside that I regularly prayed to be like him when I grew up.

That façade came crashing down as I learned more about the alleged spiritual and sexual abuse that several women experienced from him.

As I grappled with the shock, disappointment, and betrayal of these allegations, something else started to happen. A light came on and suddenly, so much of my everyday struggles from the last sixteen years made sense.

Since my first visit to IHOPKC, I've carried what I can only describe as an internal ticking clock of anxiety and fear. Because I was so indoctrinated with theology around "Jesus' imminent return," I always felt like time was running out, or that I was never going to measure up to the person God destined me to be. This was most pronounced in my spiritual life, but it also manifested in every other area. I consistently placed unrealistic expectations on myself. When I inevitably failed to meet them, it sent me into a deep existential crisis. This cycle happened multiple times a year, for years on end.

As I began to unpack my experience at IHOPKC, I was able to identify these experiences as religious trauma. I didn't experience sexual abuse while I was there, but it was a potent example of how Mike Bickle's hidden duplicity and manipulation affected the entire culture. With the help of counseling and connecting with other spiritual trauma survivors, I was finally able to put these pieces together and begin healing.

This book is a direct result of that healing process. Writing poetry became an outlet for me to express the anger, grief, betrayal, and sadness I was feeling. Many of these poems come from the raw edge of that pain, but their presence here is proof that I've made it beyond those moments into a steadier, more hopeful place.

This process also led me to a renewed faith, a path I could only find by passing through the darkness of my past. As the patron saint of pop music, Taylor Swift, says, "Looking backward might be the only way to move forward," and I've found that to be profoundly true.

Before you jump into what this book is, I do want to set some context for what it is not. It is not intended to shame or judge anyone, nor is it a blanket statement for everyone's experience at IHOPKC. It's also not intended to make any factual claims about the organization or individuals involved beyond my own percep- tions and recollections. While many have found solace and purpose in IHOPKC's mission, my experience, as detailed in this book, was complex and ultimately led to my departure.

Regardless of your experience, I simply ask that you approach the following pages with an open heart. Overall, I'm here to shine a light on spiritual abuse, manipulation, and the delicate process of healing from that. Even though IHOPKC is my specific context, my hope is that these words can be a balm to anyone reading who's experienced spiritual abuse.

To get the most out of this book, I'd recommend reading it sequentially, moving from one section to the next. It mirrors my journey of joining IHOPKC, what I experienced there, the pain it left me with, and the healing I've found through reclaiming my faith and holding others accountable. Following this journey from start to finish will offer a three-dimensional picture of a cult survivor's experience.

Lastly, please give yourself whatever space and time you need to process the topics covered in this book. Some may be emotion- ally heavy or triggering, so I wouldn't recommend reading it all in one sitting if you begin to feel those things. Be kind to yourself, take a break, go for a walk, call a friend, journal, have a good cry. So many of us who survived these communities were conditioned to neglect our bodies and feelings, but now you have full permission to honor whatever it is that you need. For additional support, I've also included a list of resources in the back of this book.

Thank you for stepping into these pages with me. I am deeply humbled that you would welcome my words into your sacred interior world. My prayer is that they validate your own feelings so that you too can find healing on the other side.

With love and hope,
Brittany

Part One
Down the Rabbit Hole

"In another moment down went Alice after it,
never once considering how in the world she was to get out again."

WHITE RABBIT

He swept through
my innocence
like a manic fever dream —
Luring me with wonder,
and his frenzied energy.

Ticking clock in hand,
he boldly exclaimed,
Join the choice elect!
Before
it's too late!

So down the rabbit hole I went,
imbued with blind allegiance.

Spellbound to the pulse
of his
holy
ticking
cadence.

YOU HAD ME AT…

God's divine call
for the
best of the bloodlines.

This elite invitation,
qualified by
angelic visitation.

Securing the truly faithful,
the ones who'd leave it all
on the field.

Burning and shining away,
till the prophecy
was fulfilled.

For God has now resolved
to change the understanding
and expression,
of our lukewarm faith,
in one generation.

3535

Thirty-five, thirty-five
East Red Bridge Road —
An unassuming address, that became
my second home.

Head
south
from
the
city,

>   at exit 182 take a
>   right,
>   follow
>   Red
>   Bridge
>   Road
>   to the place,
>   that promised the
>   Divine.

Don't let the strip mall fool you,
or question its clout.
Its reach is *International*.
There's no reason to
doubt.

MARY OF BETHANY

Mary had her alabaster flask.[1]
I, the earthen vessel of my youth.
You said, *Come and break it open.*
Worship rising as perfume.

You warned of accusations,
of being tested and tried —
Why this waste of adoration,
when there's so much more to life?

Your faith and firm conviction
convinced me to commit.
Affirming my decision,
to waste my life
for this.

---

1. See Matthew 26:6-13

SERVANT GIRL ON HER KNEES

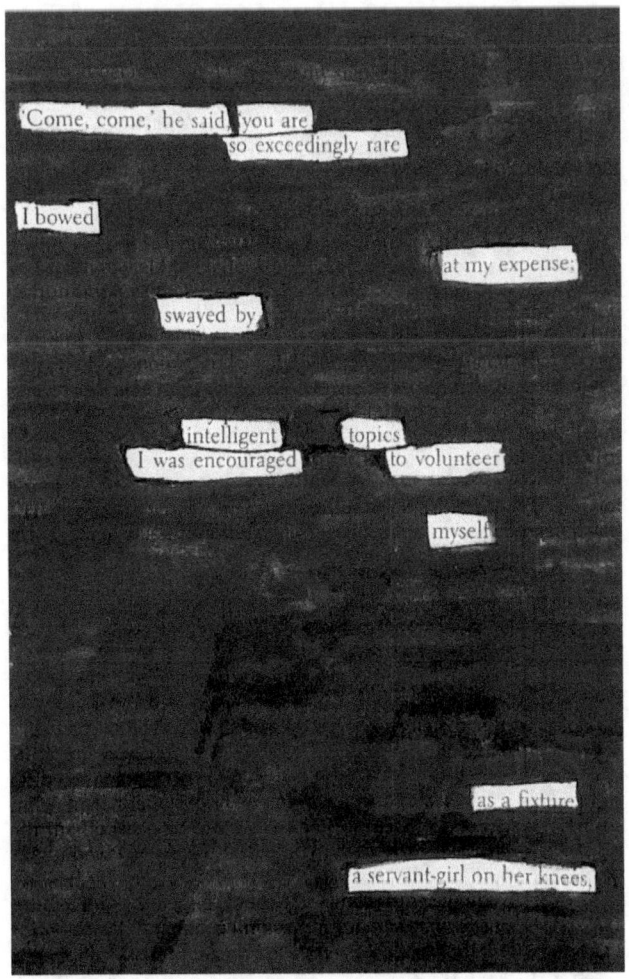

Come, come, he said.
You are so exceedingly rare.
I bowed at my expense.
Swayed by intelligent topics,
I was encouraged to volunteer myself
as a fixture.
A servant-girl on her knees.

I WANT YOU

for God's End-Time Army!
Make your home in our barracks
instead of a family.

Our war-cries
and lore will give your life meaning.

Take your place on the wall!
Keep our lamps burning!

MATTHEW 11:28-30 (A CULT LEADER'S VERSION)

Come to
me
all who are young and eager,
and I will give you a destiny to claim.

Come hear
my
dreams of grandeur, from
chariots of flame.

I'm
the chosen vessel —
Yoke yourself to
me.
This will not be light work.
You must stay close to succeed.

EASY SELL

It didn't take much
for me to give you everything.

THE REAPING

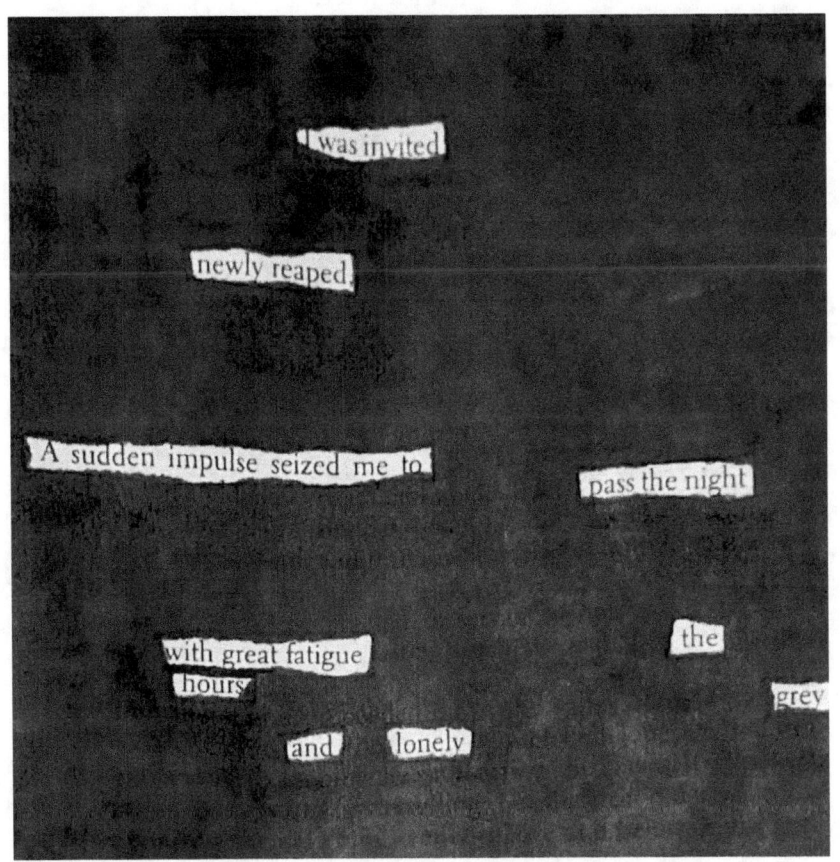

I was invited —
Newly reaped.
A sudden impulse seized me
to pass the night with great fatigue.
The hours grey,
and lonely.

ARRESTED

I didn't have the chance to dream
of what I wanted,
or where I was going.

I was barely a seed.

With soil soft and rich
from the fall of newfound grace,
their words went down smoothly,
as they mingled with the rain.

Promising potential, and wonders unseen.

Their clarion call
of the greatest of all,
arrested the worthlessness, in me.

ONE THING

It began with a phone call
disrupting
ordinary life.

They're like a Christian-Coldplay!

Intrigued, I wire in —
Mystified by this bold claim
that's slowly proving true.

Presence
fills my room,
carried by musical offerings
of power, and praise.

A swooping pan reveals
an earthly reflection
of the heavenly seascape
around the Throne.

Thousands upon thousands,
consumed
with passionate fervor, for
OneThing.

In an instant, I decide.

Whatever this is,
Wherever this is,
I have to be there.

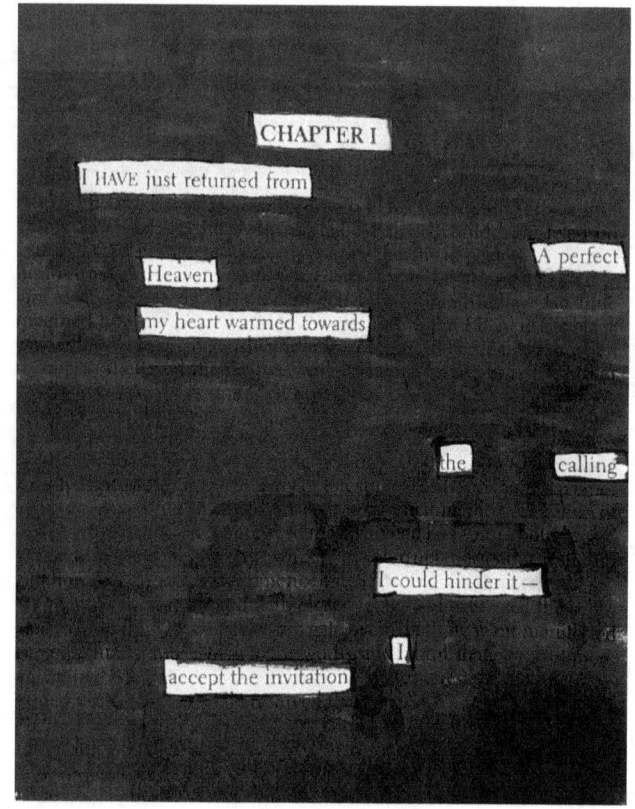

CHAPTER 1
I have just returned
from a perfect heaven.
My heart warmed towards the calling.
I could hinder it —
I accept the invitation.

Part Two
Makings of a Mad House

"What sort of people live about here?" "In that direction," the Cat said, waving its right paw round, "lives a Hatter: and in that direction," waving the other paw, "lives a March Hare. Visit either you like: they're both mad."

"But I don't want to go among mad people," Alice remarked. "Oh, you can't help that," said the Cat: "we're all mad here."

MAD HATTER

A sanctified tea party
on perpetual loop.
With madness and riddles
by the Hatter, in blue.

I take my seat at his table, the clock frozen at six.
Ensuring endless devotion, amidst
parlor tricks.

Everything is obscure.

Nothing makes sense.

But instead of challenging the chaos,
I sip tea, without end.

NEURODEVELOPMENT, OR THE LACK THEREOF

With the rose colored hues
of my supple young mind,
I couldn't discern,
the real from the sublime.

As far as I knew, they were one in the same.
What could go wrong?

Aren't all prophets insane?

PRAYER ROOM ETIQUETTE

Take a seat (but leave a space)
between you

and your neighbor.

God forbid the place you choose,
already belongs to another.

Sing along or read the Word.
Sit and sway or walk the aisles.
Let your incense fill the air,
Mic in hand for rapid fire.

Make sure you're almost screaming,
We just ask you God!
Never mind the lack of windows.
We have all the Light
you'll want.

Two hours of daily prayer.
Fasting twice a week.
These were the pious tenets
I abided
as a teen.

Be a faithful witness.
Do not waver from the truth.
Take all your youthful vigor
and waste it here in
solitude.

This charge, it promised
purpose.
An ancient path to the holy.

Who was I to question?
What more was there for me?

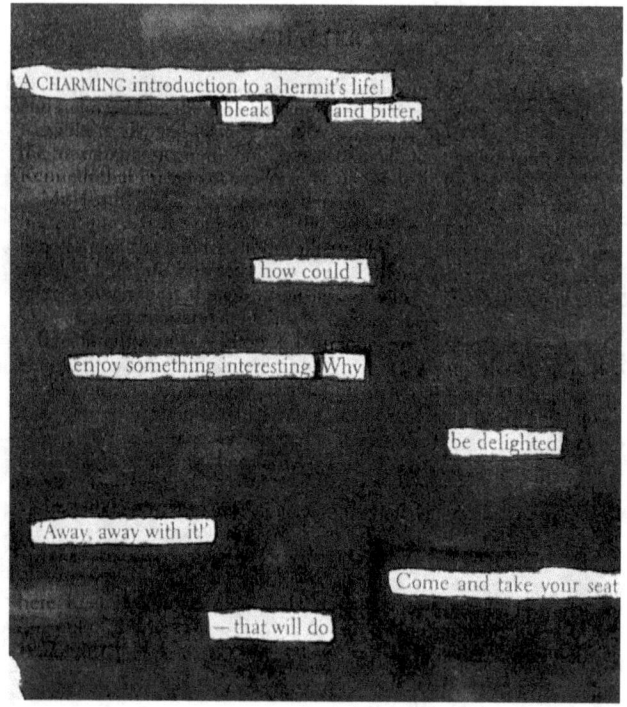

A charming introduction to a hermit's life!
Bleak and bitter.
How could I enjoy something interesting?
Why be delighted?
Away, away with it!
Come and take your seat —
That will do.

FORERUNNERS

Forerunner This.
Forerunner That.
Branding our souls
Like a cold hard fact.

Day and Night.
Night and Day.
We shut ourselves in.
Glued to grey chairs,
that become our second skin.

Feeding on fury
without caution or tact —
We embrace the one, true calling.

To lead and prepare
the third act.

ABSTAIN

Abstain, reject, consecrate —
Preserve yourself for a better way.

Rest your eyes beneath my shade,
surrendered to
this sacred
waste.

Hush, hush!
Run, run!
Keep fast, keep fast!
No, no.

WHY SO SERIOUS?

Furrowed brows
are screaming loud
of sanctified sobriety.

Somber frowns
etching our vows
of youthful piety.

QUESTIONS FOR THE END OF THE WORLD

Should I get married or go to college?

Should I have kids?

Should we take care of the earth,
if it'll just be made new again?

Is it okay for me to have fun?

Am I doing enough?

Do regular jobs matter?

Will I survive, when it's tough?

Is it okay for me to watch movies?

Will I be safe?

Could I withstand torture, if I'm punished for my faith?

NAMELESS & FACELESS

I arrive to the party
willingly, shedding my name.
Donning a mask
to cover my face.

A face full of wonder.
A face altogether lovely.
Who became a blank slate
with unwavering, fealty.

I dance and I mingle,
staying far from the blaze
that borders the edges,
ensuring we remain.

With rhythmic devotion,
I pass the time
two by two.
Giving all that I am,
to this masquerade
of truth.

INTERIOR GLOOM

I must not eat.
I wish to be troubled by nobody —
Today I am turned
to interior gloom.

CONFESSIONS OF A TEENAGE CULT MEMBER

To whom shall we go?
Why would we leave?
For only you and your words
have the purpose we seek.

Through grandiose visions,
we've come to believe.
You are the Head,
of God's faithful elite.

THE FIRE ON THE ALTAR

Others can,
but you can not.
You must pave the way,
through voluntary want.
Surrendering dreams
and worldly desires,
to uphold and maintain
the altar of fire.
Its incessant flames
raging
night and day.
Without care or concern,
for who's scorched along the way.

NO, NOT THE PANCAKE HOUSE

You won't find pancake stacks
or buttery decadence here.
You won't find much food at all —
The end is near.

Instead of tables and chairs
where bellies are filled,
these seats hold
the hungry.
Those set apart, for His will.

It's this hallowed ground
where praise rises nonstop,
that we mean when we say,
we go to IHOP.

BITTER/SWEET

I sit beneath your shade
thinking I stumbled upon
a feast.

Eating freely of your scrolls
that hold the the bitter, and the sweet.

Ravenous desperation
makes it impossible to leave.

So without hesitation, I take the fruit
you offer me.

CIVILIZED

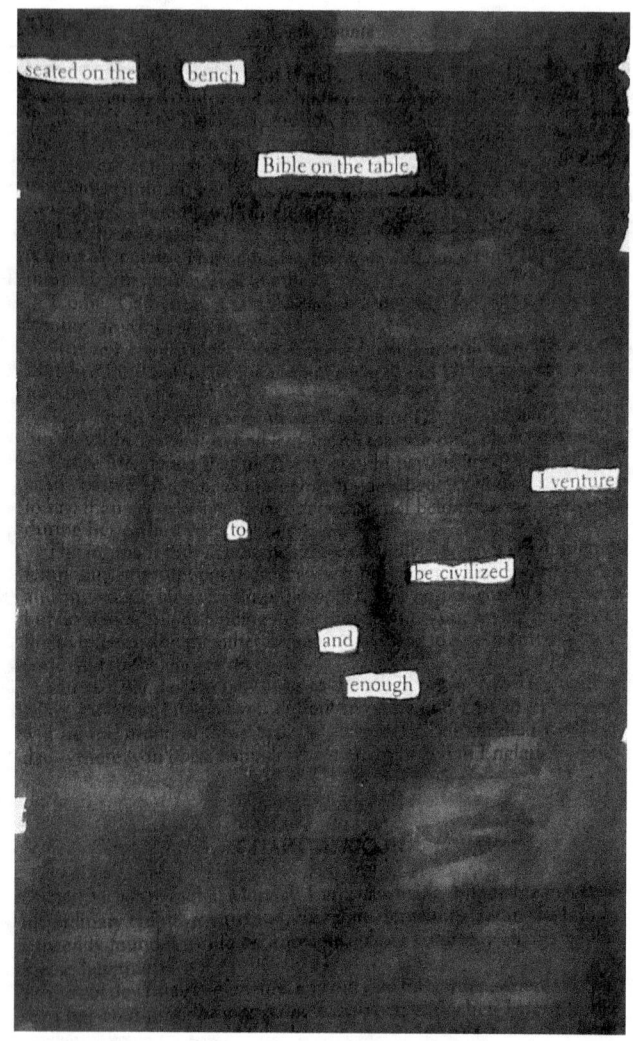

Seated on the bench.
Bible on the table.
I venture to be civilized,
and enough.

SATURDAY, BUT MAKE IT APOCALYPTIC

I memorize your seals and bowls.
Convinced your infallible insight,
was worth more than gold.

I fear your portrait of the Man in Red.
Thinking it normal
to live today for the end.

Every Saturday.
Week after week.
Without fault or error.
I recite it all, on repeat.

THE PACERS

Back and forth,
we tear up the rug.
Back and forth,
without all the fun.

Back and forth,
Is something wrong with me?
Back and forth,
Why can't I just sit still and read?

Back and forth,
I claim this carpeted aisle.
Back and forth,
rarely breaking a smile.

PRAYER PAWN

I come and go
again and again.

Caught in your orbit
of incense and worship.

An innocent pawn in your game.

IS THIS A CULT?

Oh, I promise you, it's not.

Why would a cult leader
teach us their signs
and vain plots?

So we're told we're special.

Is that a crime?
Doesn't that reflect
the heart of the Divine?

No one's forcing us to stay.

God is just doing something new.
There is no greater purpose
than staying here,
in this room.

Why go anywhere else?
Why would we leave?
When so much heavenly promise
affirms a man's dream?

Part Three
Lost

"You're not the same as you were before...You've lost your muchness."

WHO

R

U

like a fragrance on the wind,
this query passes freely.
my answer just as hollow,
as the haze that questions me.

desperately searching,
i try to find an answer.
but all this shrinking and this growing,
has warped what was remembered.

i can't give what you ask for,
or the answers you seek.
i can't explain myself i'm afraid,
because i'm not myself, you see.

IHOP GIRL

she sits in the corner and passes the time,
with harmonized songs repeating in rhyme.

she molds her young essence and meter of speech,
after vehement prayers, screamed on repeat.

her weekends forgo teenage reveries,
to secure and appease foreboding anxiety.

authentic desire and heartfelt devotion,
intwine with a mission that leads to erosion —

an erosion of self, and all rational thought.
of the girl
who didn't even know

she was lost.

DRINK ME

i drank of your words
to make myself small.
till none of me was left.
nothing, at all.

AM I BRUISED?

wincing in surprise,
i turn, i twist and spin.
to find the violet hues,
peppering my skin.

with numbing horror
and denial,
i fall swiftly to the ground.
afraid to face the truth,
as memories
compound.

NONSENSE

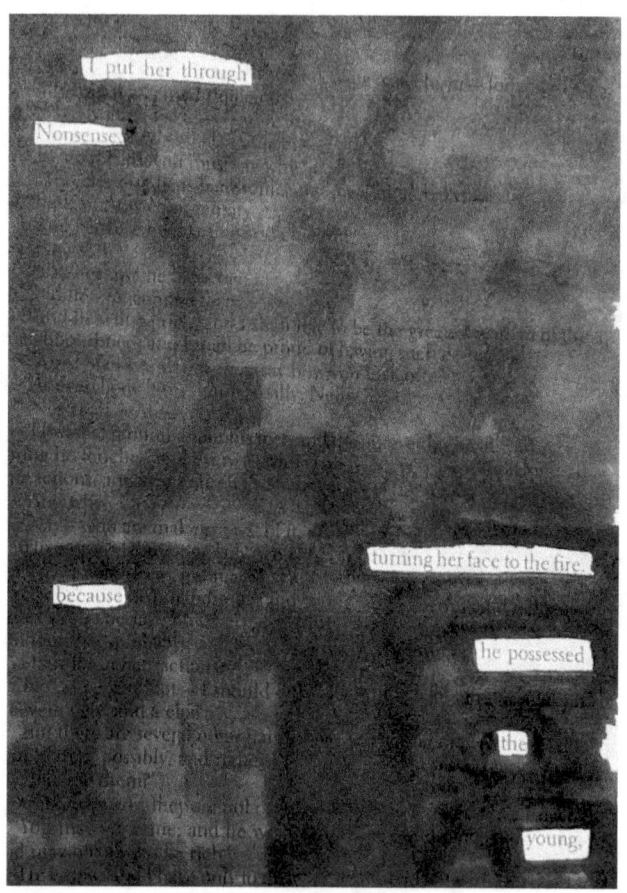

i put her through
nonsense.
turning her face to the fire,
because he possessed
the young.

STRIPPED

a strip mall was fitting
for your reverent brigade,
that stripped bare my instincts,
securing blind faith.

RED BRIDGE ROAD

travel with me
   down old red bridge road.
      where i locked my love
         around rusting steel, that told

of a path to greatness
   should i join in its steps.
      down the crimson trail.
         a path, splattered red.

a sacrifice of self
   freely given to the stream.
      no matter how steep the price
         or how violent, our screams.

it's here I held firm
   till I cried with a plea,
      for this binding to break
         and secure, my release.

MAKE IT STOP

his ticking clock
and doomsday watch
once kept my heart in check.

but now his weighty pins and gears,
are shackled 'round my neck.

it shows no mercy for my frailty.

keeping tabs
with
every
tick.

ever taunting and accessing,
like some cruel incessant trick.

each new day feels like a failure.
like i'm already behind.
who can save me from this torture?
who can stop the hands of time?

GOOD

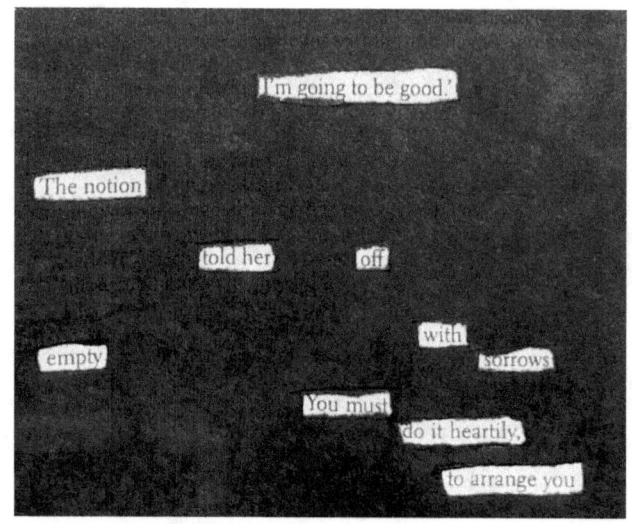

i'm going to be good.
the notion told her off
with empty sorrows.

you must do it heartily,
to arrange you.

WHAT IF?

what if everything i could attain and be,
slowly wastes away, behind the scenes?

what if my ambitions and silent screams,
echo into a void, that no one sees?

will my life be empty?
will his bad omen come true?
will the shame and disappointment,
fill me through and through?

SPIRITUAL VIOLENCE

when you said
the violent take it by force,[1]
i didn't think you meant
that's how you'd take me.

---

1. See Matthew 11:12

HOLY HUNGER

if only i'd chosen pancakes over prayer rooms.
at least then i would have never gone hungry.

WHAT MUST I DO?

if i plan out every moment,
fill each day with solemn tears,
if i scream louder,
will You be moved to hear?

SHATTERED

ninety-five pounds
were all that remained,
from the blood-beaten path
of their holy hunger games.

designed to test
and weed out the weak,
so all that remained,
were the faithful elite.

i welcomed this loss
of spirit
body
and soul.

until I finally shattered,
beneath
their control.

I RIDE A FEW WORDS

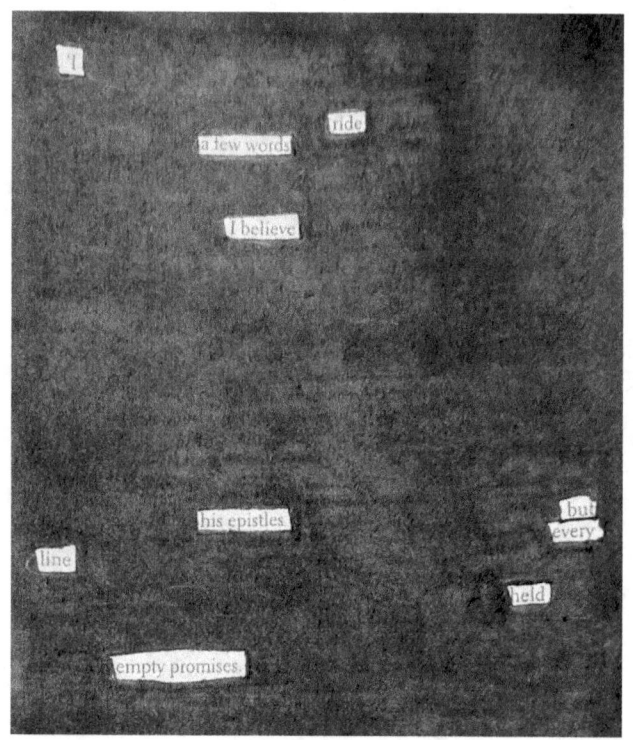

i ride a few words.
i believe his epistles.
but every line
held empty promises.

TIMES NEW ROMAN

i never knew i could be
haunted
by italics and serifs —
this bolded language with feet
chasing me down like a sheriff.

locking me behind bars
and shackling my bones.
keeping me hostage
with stylized drones.

POSEIDON'S FURY

i thought i caught the right stream.
that i was swimming in the right direction.
but i'd been captured —
caught in the rip tide of poseidon's fury.

i was a prisoner kept beneath his kingdom.
waking beneath the water
without gills to withstand this depth.
this pressure.
this world without air.

WASHED

your vision.
your dream.
your fantasy.
tore through my life,
washing away all of me.

HINDSIGHT

i should have known
from a room adorned with seats of grey,
that my effervescent spectrum,
would soon fade away.

DESPERATE WISHES

all i want
is to let go
of this hold you have on me.
to cast it on the millstone,[1]
that takes you out to sea.

---

1. See Matthew 18:6

CANCELED NOISE

suddenly, everything is too loud.

every decibel a crucible,
replaying trauma on loop.

my brain screams danger.
my body retreats.

canceled noise
my only haven,
and solace of peace.

CHIEF OF MY GRIEFS

they asked for all of you
and i didn't hesitate.

emptying you of your youth
for their devout escapades.

i had no way of knowing.
no way to foresee.

that forfeiting you for their vision,
would be chief
of my griefs.

IN THE NAME OF ALL THAT FEELS

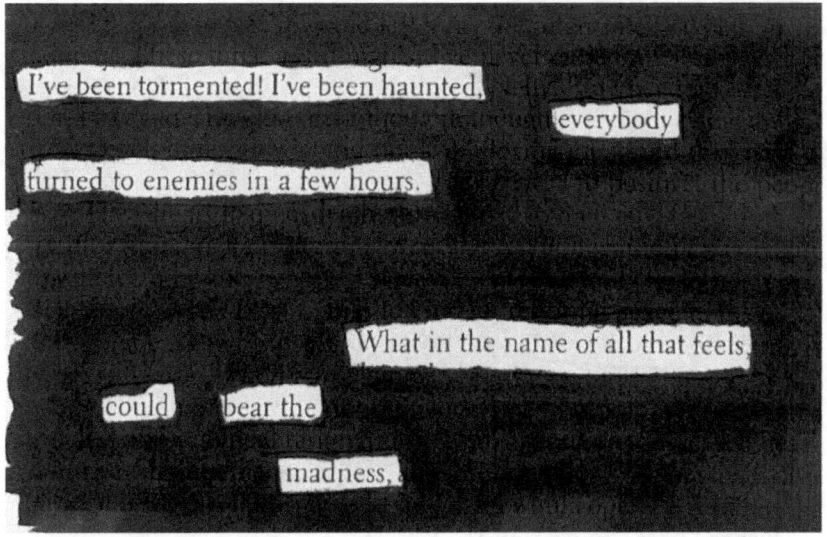

i've been tormented! i've been haunted!
everybody turned to enemies in a few hours.
what in the name of all that feels
could bear the madness?

THE PROTECTOR

i locked you away
with impenetrable shields.
my fear like a ward, keeping you
captive for years.

i thought i was helping.
that i was protecting you.
from the merciless prowler,
that hid from your view.

i'm stuck in that story, of what was
and could be.
afraid to unbind

these restraints,
lest the past should repeat.

EMPTY ANSWERS

you know something's tragically wrong when someone asks,

what do you like to do for fun?

and you can't think of one task.

I'D LIKE A REFUND PLEASE

i recounted the cost,
went through my receipts.

there's no way in hell,
this was worth a front seat.

PSALM 27:4

when i read about the onething,
the pressure falls like instinct.

holding remnants of your ghost
that terrorized my youth.
walking through my walls,
under the guise of twisted truth.

it's too potent right now.
too reminiscent of your poison.
so i'll go the long way 'round,
till i can rid this weary burden.

IRONY

you said our biggest fear would be regret.
but the only thing i now lament,
is trusting every word you said.

WIPED

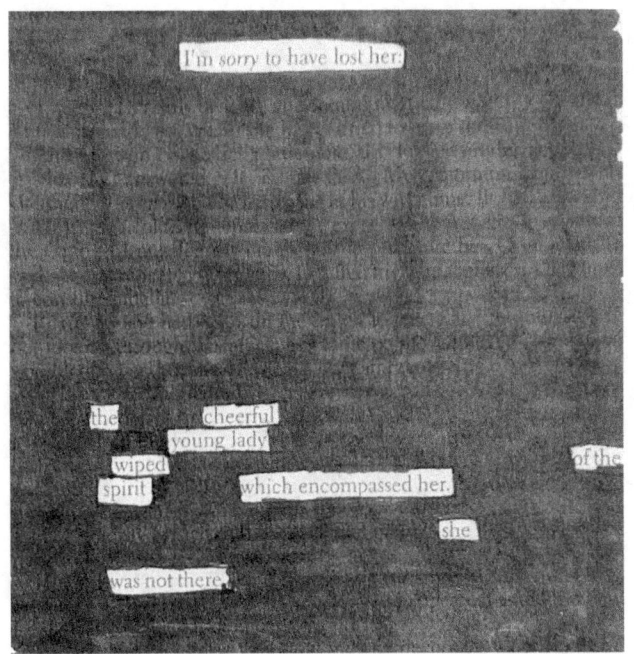

i'm sorry to have lost her.

the cheerful young lady,
wiped of the spirit
which encompassed her.

she was not there.

TRANSLATOR

god in heaven,
translator of my deepest sighs —

help.

Part Four
Defiant Awakening

"Wake up, Alice dear!" said her sister;
"Why, what a long sleep you've had!"

HOUSE OF ~~PRAYER~~ CARDS

I thought this place was stable,
an impenetrable domain.
But now I shout along with Alice,
and join her bold refrain.

Who cares for all your tirades?
You're nothing but a pack of cards!
Damned to tumble and fall quickly,
for all your actions, in the dark.

THE WOES

Woe to you,
and your vile hypocrisy.
Polished and spruced
to maintain your theocracy.

For behind all your lies
and falsified schemes,
lies the spoiled rotten truth,
and everything unclean.

DOUBLE LIFE

Shock me now,
don't shock me later,
was your constant humble plea.

All while living a double life, of
violating schemes.

DUALISTIC FRUIT

The fruit was both
sweet and rotten
at the same time.

It went down easy.
Eagerly.
Willingly.

With no stench or odor
to give away its decay.

Its half-life was long.
Quiet.
Calculated.

Deceptive in its goodness.

Till the appointed time
when my unraveling,
unmasked reality.

RANSACKED

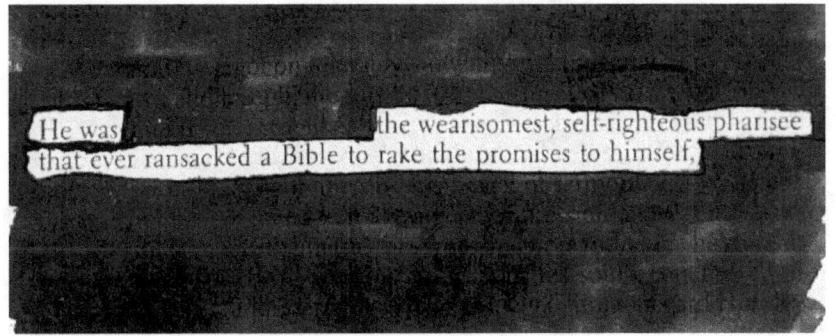

He was
the wearisomest,
self-righteous pharisee,
that ever ransacked a Bible
to rake promises, to himself.

SEEDS OF REPAIR

Some days I can't deal
with this cycle of agony.

These ups and these downs,
between healing
and tragedy.

The more that I know,
the more I want to scream.
To weep for the girl
who fell prey
to his schemes.

But I know in my core
that this turbulent path,
sows the seeds
of repair, as I
empty
my
wrath.

AN ACRONYM ACROSTIC

I
Hope there's an
Ounce of decency that finds its way, into your
Pent up
Kaleidoscope of
Clandestine
Games.
Because though you have no
Fear of consequence in your present state,
Fire is promised, without debate.
Combusting myths and falsified
Fables, that you
Forced down our throats while
Masking your labels, of quiet
Assault and hidden agendas,
Found alongside your
Secret vendettas.
Much could be lost as you
Go through the flames,
Producing only ashes, from
Rotted wood and hay.

KING DAVID IS NOT A COP OUT

They say you're not your sin.
That David fell and was restored.
That you can do as you please,
with your mantle still secured.

But they forget about the prophet,
who confronts the vain king.
Promising violent repercussions,
for all his lustful,
selfish schemes.[1]

---

1. See 2 Samuel 12:7-12

SIDE ROOM VIOLATIONS

Darkness swirls
and hides its face,
in side rooms filled
with devious ways.

That silence the broken,
violated and vulnerable.
All to appear, as righteous
and honorable.

DECEIVED

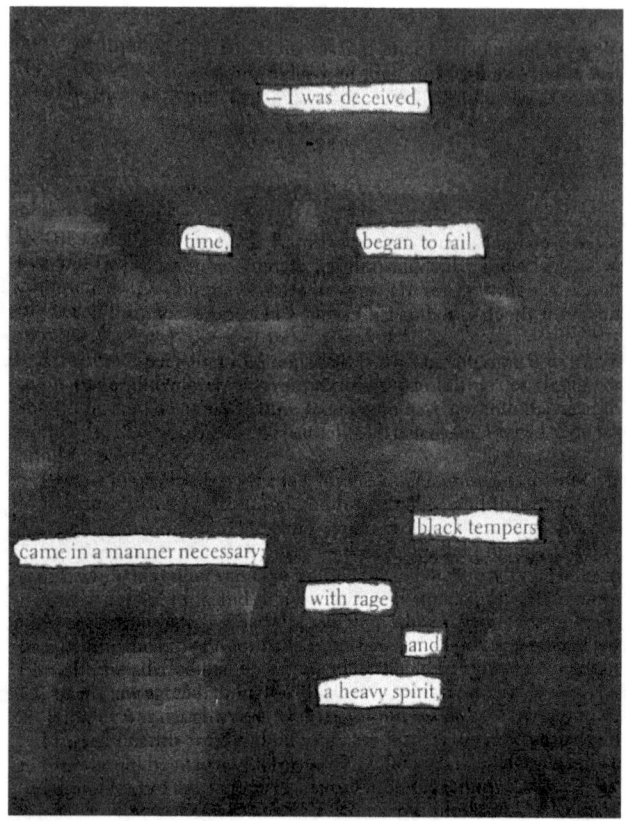

I was deceived.
Time began to fail.
Black tempers
came in a manner necessary —
With rage,
and a heavy spirit.

GROUNDING

I look to the mountains and say on repeat,
I'm in Colorado.
I'm safe, and I'm free.

HOW MANY TIMES?

How many times
was I bowed down in worship, when
ten
feet
away
you were crushing a spirit?

How many times
did I make supplication,
as you berated
the broken
with merciless questions?

How many times
did I open your doors,
unaware of the evil
clothed as something pure?

OLD MAN

Since you want to uphold
your canonized mythology,
you'd do well
to revisit
the foreboding prophecies.

Of turmoil and harm
you'd cause to the innocent.
Through selfish desires
and ruthless, impatience.

WICKS

It was us who burned —
Who surrendered our wicks.
To your delusional altar,
of dogmatic tricks.

WHAT I WISH SOMEONE TOLD ME

Broken open as an offering.
Poured out and sweet.

That's precious.
Pure.
So very rare to see.

Just remember the God of the small —

Beauty and magic woven into the seams.
Of your talents.
passions,
and spirited dreams.

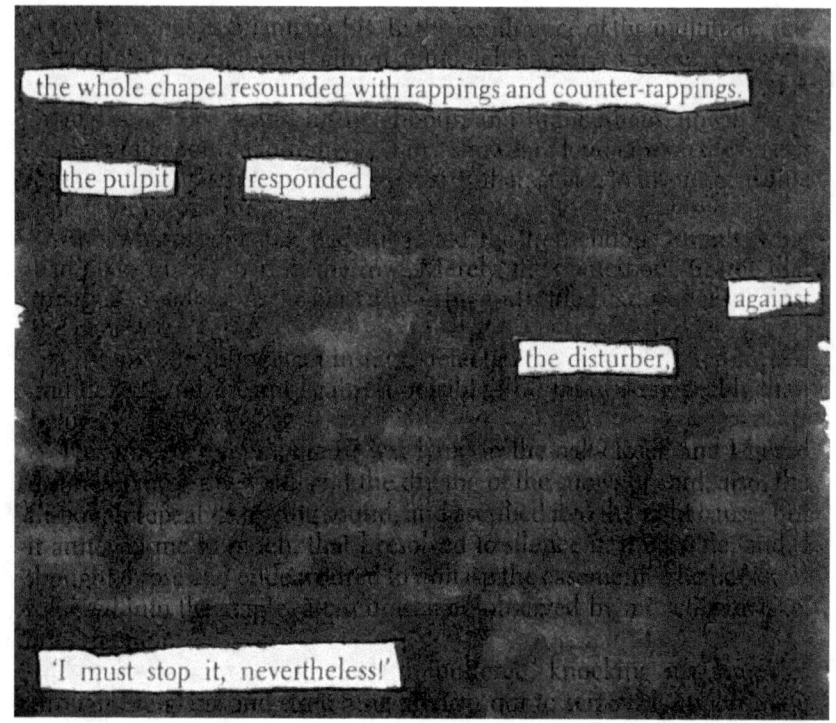

The whole chapel resounded with rappings
and counter-rappings.
The pulpit responded against the disturber.
I must stop it, nevertheless!

DUPED

Realizing the wool was pulled over your eyes
while you thought you grazed in safety,
is like not knowing you were hypnotized,
and waking from your sleeping.

T O R N A D O A L L E Y

I just think it's ironic that we attributed

divine protection to a cyclone

incarnate, hell-bent

on destroying

everything

in its

path, to

serve

its

reality.

TO THE CANARIES

With a foresight we could not perceive,
your songs filled the dark.
Imploring us
to see.

Through shallow breaths
your claims rang true.
But we called you bitter,
put the blame on you.

We plugged up our ears
from your merciful warnings.
Now with hindsight we plead,
forgive us our scorning.

SEALED

We were sealed for
your protection,
and bound to submission.
Taught to stay in line
and never, to question.

Shutting us in
with your righteous façade.
Our wholehearted allegiance,
your greatest con.

Till your merciless ploys
and heavenly ruse,
exposed and revealed, the
devastating
truth.

Come home
and establish a table.
Quiet, altered,
and favorable.

18 REASONS WHY MATTHEW 18 DOESN'T APPLY TO CLERGY SEXUAL ABUSE

1. A victim should never meet alone with their abuser.
2. A victim should never meet alone with their abuser.
3. A victim should never meet alone with their abuser.
4. A victim should never meet alone with their abuser.
5. A victim should never meet alone with their abuser.
6. A victim should never meet alone with their abuser.
7. A victim should never meet alone with their abuser..
8. A victim should never meet alone with their abuser.
9. A victim should never meet alone with their abuser.
10. A victim should never meet alone with their abuser.
11. A victim should never meet alone with their abuser.
12. A victim should never meet alone with their abuser.
13. A victim should never meet alone with their abuser.
14. A victim should never meet alone with their abuser.
15. A victim should never meet alone with their abuser.
16. A victim should never meet alone with their abuser.
17. A victim should never meet alone with their abuser.
18. A victim should never meet alone with their abuser.

I could keep going, if that's what you'd prefer.

DEN OF THIEVES

He binds and He ties
strips of rugged leather[1],
for every soul that was stripped
by their pious, endeavors.

Pulsing vengeance and zeal
rush through His veins.
As every table flips
like the ruthless, tempest waves.

---

1. See John 2:15

TICKING CLOCK

You cut off my hand
and swallowed my prime.
Even now it haunts me —
the ticking of time.

Will the gears stop moving?
Will I be here when it counts?
Will I reach my potential,
before time runs out?

There's no way of knowing,
so I scurry and scatter.
Following every word,
unaware how I shatter.

This is the price.
This is the cost.
No matter the breaking.
No matter what's lost.

But then there's a pull.
A tether deep within.
Your madness and chatter,
fades like a dream.

This new voice is kind.
It's gentle and soft.
It bends low and whispers,
There's no hands on the clock.

FELLOW-MARTYRS

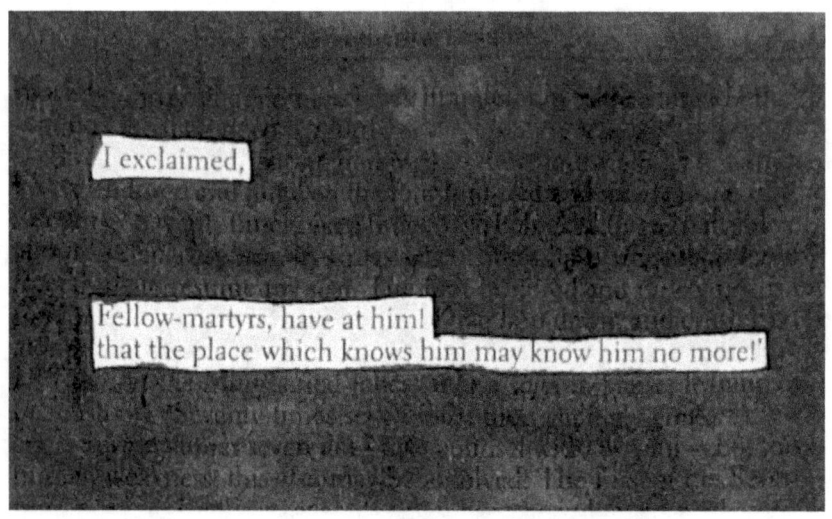

I exclaimed,
Fellow-martyrs, have at him!
That the place which knows him
may know him no more!

HOLY SHIT

What do I do,
with all of this "holy" shit?
Guess I'll till the ground,
try and plant seeds in it —
Of peace.
Calm.
All that was stripped.

Maybe new life will grow.
As I sort, through the thick of it.

LOVE BOMBS

I didn't think to run for cover
from the air raids
of your love.
Slipping through my defenses,
with the
meekness, of a dove.

Its metronomic fury
beat with unrelenting blaze.
Mesmerized, I stood unflinching.
Despite the threat
to my fate.

The sirens started shrieking.
My family warned and yelled.
Begging me to
find safety.
Pleading, to no avail.

How could I step away?
What need is there to flee?
When this explosive love,
chose and
wanted me?

Digging in my heels,
I doubled down and remained.
Blind to the affliction
of this distorted faith.

Years later past the wreckage,
in skies that now know peace,
I still tear out the shrapnel
from being broken at the knees.

If only I'd run for cover.
If only I'd seen the signs.
Maybe I'd have fewer scars.
Maybe I could have lit up my own sky.

UNWELCOMED WARNINGS

I sit with my coffee, anxiously bouncing my knees.
Knowing I'm not exactly the person, she's expecting to meet.

Her I know well, and that's what makes this so hard.
Because I remember her trusting, and wide-open heart.

How do you tell a devoted younger you,
the devastating reality, and soul-crushing truth?

That the man she looks up to and highly esteems,
is a devious wolf, disguised as a sheep?

That the place where she worships and longs to fit in,
holds unfathomable evil, and a multitude of sins?

I do my best to be gentle as I begin to speak,
but her defense rises quickly, in scoffing disbelief.

I know I can't stop her, or force her to stay.
So I trust in the Goodness, following her through the fray.

The fray that's soon coming.

That fray already at work.

The fray she'll soon conquer, and bravely usurp.[1]

---

1. Inspired by Jennae Cecelia's poem, "I Met My Younger Self For Coffee."

A CLEAR HEAD WAS YOUR GREATEST THREAT

You said to stay hungry.
Weak at the knees.
In the name of devotion
I willingly, agreed.

When we fast and we pray, the Spirit gives more.
It's all for love, you claimed.
To wholeheartedly adore.

All this you did, to
keep me from

thinking.

Lest I shake off the fog
and wake, from my sleeping.

THE LIMIT DOES NOT EXIST

An exciting opportunity
is soon overpowered,
by the fear of my limits.
Time's threat to expire.

It plays out as a tiresome,
frenetic labor craze,
that echoes the urgency,
of fleeting dying days.

Must go faster.
Must recklessly speed.
For impending disaster
is closer, than you think.

I maniacally swerve and
adopt a lead foot.
Till quiet assurance,
subdues
all my *shoulds.*

Reminding my taunting
unfeasible lists,
It's okay to move slow.
The limit does not exist.

HAMBURGER HELPER

With gilded resolve
you claimed to critique,
the flavorful pretense,
of embellished meat.

When all along
you continued to brew,
deceptive extracts
of artificial, truth.

We partook with pleasure.
Unaware of the toxins,
that coursed through our veins
of eager, devotion.

CENTER

Take space and weep.

Between the porch of fallen heroes
and the altar of our grief.

Breathe in, breathe out.

For in the rising and the falling
we find peace, amidst our doubts.

COLLATERAL DAMAGE

The trouble with building the ship at sea,
is that you use the bodies of your crew,
to shore up the holes
as you sink.

THE HOLIDAY

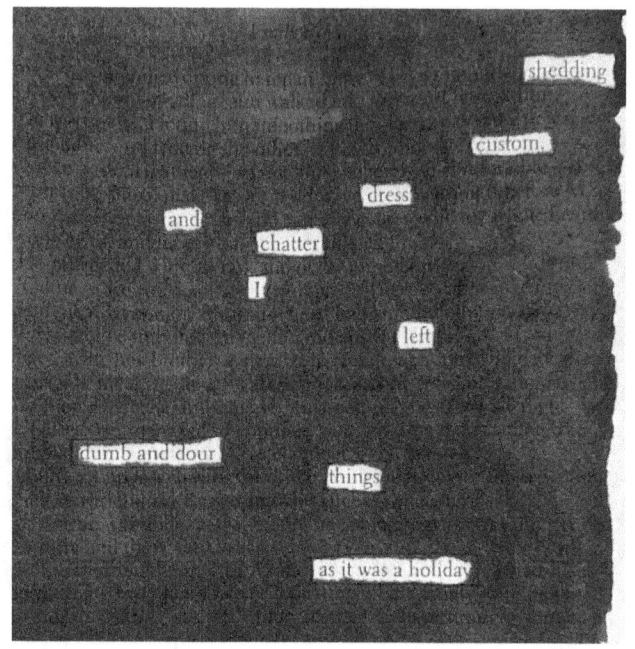

Shedding custom, dress,
and chatter,
I left dumb and dour things
as it was a holiday.

DEAR CELLULITE

For most of my life, I didn't have much of you around.
I was small, petite.
Always lacking in pounds.

Some of this was normal, simple genetics
at play.
Till I forced your eviction,
when I fasted
for days.

Give me a chance to explain —

I was promised this hunger,
this voluntary want,
would give me steadfast love.
Special access, to God.

With a white knuckled grip,
you resolved
to hold on.
No matter how hard I tried,
the weight
never, stayed on.

Looking back, it's more clear.
What led you to flee.
You were sensing the danger
that I couldn't see.

Until recently.

When I first noticed
your return,
I wasn't entirely pleased.
I blame that on our world
and the patriarchy.

But then one day,
I was struck with relief.
Realizing you're
here,
because I'm
finally
safe.

So I just wanted you to know,
I'm glad you're here to stay.
Because you're a plush reminder,
that I'm at peace, and okay.

TO THOSE THAT WERE SAFE

O Captain! My Captain! We came with hearts undone,
By the bruising and the beating,
By the sea that raged and won,
Our weary hopes on thinning ropes,
Were remnants of our charter,
With stumbling steps we found a home,
The vessel safe and fostered;

    O heart! Heart! Heart!
        Remember the grinding tread,
            Where on the deck my heart revived,
                No longer cold and dead.

O Captain! My Captain! Who taught us how to see,
The wisdom of a servant's heart,
Of building people before a dream,
With you, we found a kingdom embedded in our days,
In brewed elixirs daily given, in the straws we threw away;

    Hear Captain! dear leader!
        Our thanks woven like a thread,
            It's a dream that we were spared the fray
                Of falling cold and dead.

Though of my joys, I could not answer,
My lips grown pale and still,
My Captain lent a gentle arm, to restore my pulse and will,
Then comrades came with noble care,
To guide this voyage home,
With laughter like a gentle breeze,
We took the seas as one.

    Exult O shores, and ring O bells!

Where burdens first were shed,
　Walk the deck as one revived,
　　No longer cold and dead.[1]

---

1. Inspired by 'O Captain! My Captain!' by Walt Whitman (1865)

BLIND LEADING THE BLIND

Like babes
whose eyes had yet to open,
we felt held
and known by you.

Trusting your claims of the unseen,
as undeniable
truth.

But if our sight was clear,
we'd meet your
milky eyes.
Realizing with horror —
Your eyes were just as blind.

MOTHER KNOWS BEST

Few things are as strong
as a mother's intuition.
It cuts through bravado —
Sees right through
vain ambition.

She may not have the right words
or doctoral reflections.
But we'd do well to believe,
her intrinsic protection.

Lying deep in her veins,
latent with power.
Breaking through darkness,
to expose the prowler.

NOTHING CAN SEPARATE

There is no secular and sacred.
There is no loss in recreation.
Meaning is not defined,
by spiritual qualifications.

It all sits enshrined
by a beautiful essence.
Preserved by its Maker
with inherent goodness.

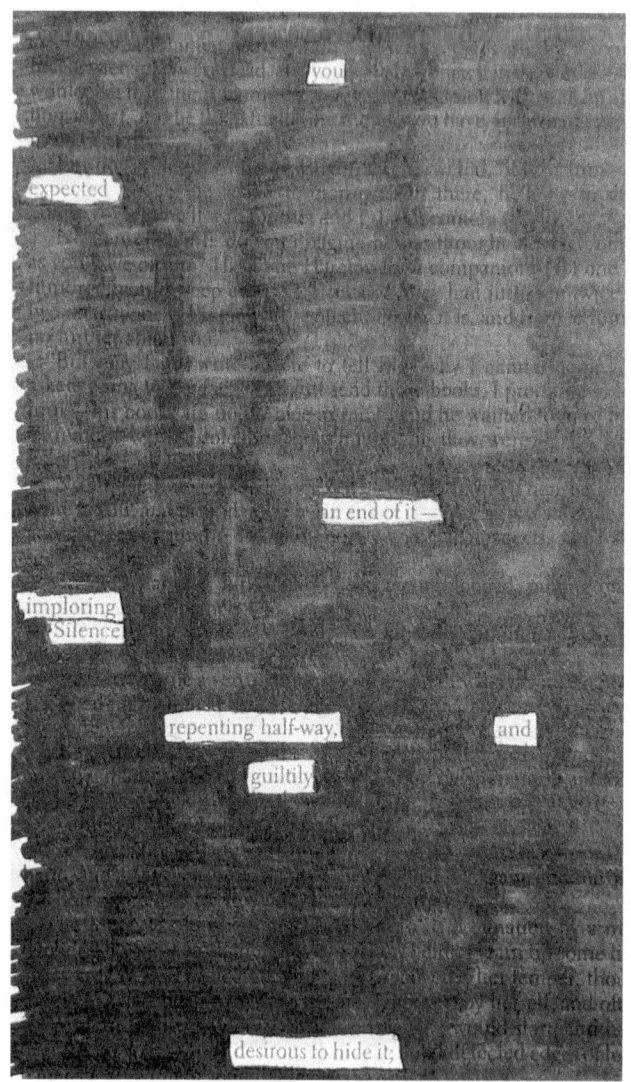

You expected an end of it —
Imploring silence.
Repenting halfway.
And guiltily desirous to hide it.

SMOKES

We were nothing but a pack of smokes to you.

Shaken and packed tightly
into your warehouse of circumvented dreams.

One was never enough.

So you kept shaking.
Packing.
Lighting us up.

Letting us shine for a moment
for your own lethal enjoyment.

GIVE ME THE ORDINARY

The morning hellos
and the routine goodbyes.
The rustle of sheets
in our ordinary nights.

With our ordinary love
be it lost, gained, or held,
by the beat of the drums
in our ordinary shells.

For it's here we find beauty,
in this paradoxical mundane.
In returning and resting,
to our ordinary days.

DARK HORSE

Keep trying to haunt us
with your dark horse of betrayal.
That makes *you* the victim
of calculated evil.

We know it's not real.
We can make out the truth.
Because that's the thing about ghosts —
We can see right through you.

TO MY GALS

I came to you battered.
I came to you bruised.
Unaware of the holy,
in glitter and booze.

In melodies sung
with wild abandon.
In Swift calculations,
and fae made by cauldrons.

In all of these things
and so, so much more.
You walked me home to myself.
You walked me home, to my core.

THIS IS GIRLHOOD

Joy crackles through me.

A force of effervescent beauty,
whose sparks fly
through the blackened night.

Illuminating places left
desolate.
The little girl, I left behind.

I lead her way back
with a glittery cadence.

Returning and resting
in girlhood's remembrance.

OPEN

Open up my eyes that I may see,
the wondrous things
of being alive,
awake,
unashamedly free.

I'LL TRADE YA

Come all who are weary,
with your gears and ticking clocks.
Come trade your heavy burdens,
for a light and easy lot.

A CHANGE IN THE EXPRESSION

The only change in the understanding
and expression of Christianity I want to see,
is a commitment to
justice, safety,
and
accountability.

.

THE RETURN OF SUNSHINE

Are you feeling better this morning?
Infinitely better.
Attentive, bending, embracing.
I learned the return of sunshine
must be for ourselves,
the chief consideration.

I SEE IT NOW

A teen that should've been enjoying
the boisterous rites of my youth.
And hell, actually eating
robust, real food.

Fear and firm conviction
kept these rigors in place.
Terrified that if I wavered
I'd lose my place, in the race.

So 'round and 'round I went,
thinking this would secure my worth.
Blind to imbedded value
that's wholly separate, from work.

USUALLY I'M CALM

But an internal torrent
runs violently beneath.
Like the billows and waves
demanding justice, and peace.

FREE FLOWING

I come to the river,
buckets in hand.
Expecting snide remarks,
or fierce reprimands.

But this bubbling current.
This generous peace.
Welcomes my messy,
imperfect routines.

It reminds me again
with an unceasing stream —
*There's no need to perform
or earn what is free.*

LOVE REDEFINED

The love I give is not conditional.
It pours out in buckets
Like promised residuals.

Freely rewarded, and never transitional.
Here for the taking.

It was never transactional.

WHEN YOUR LESSONS BACKFIRE

You taught us to cry out day and night.
So our unyielding petitions,
should come as no surprise.

DEAR JANE

I hate that the first rhyme
that comes to mind for your name, is "pain."

Your purity of heart
should have never been treated this way.

Trampled and exploited, by his weaponized faith.
That promised a calling, wrapped up in his name.

But your fearless resolve broke through the surface.
Untethering yourself from his fictional purpose.

Rewriting your story as a triumphant chorus.
As the Jane Who's Unchained, reigning victorious.

THE POWER OF A RESTED LIFE

No destiny is squandered
should you
break

from the locks.

Binding you to submission,
in fifteen minute blocks.

You will not perish.
You'll be okay.

Rest won't compromise
your vision.
You won't fall away.

WARNING SIGN

I wish I saw it.
Wish you came with a warning sign —

Proceed With Caution.
Beware Steep Incline.

I followed your markers.
Flagged down
by your cadence,
of promised potential
through fire, and fragrance.

The road never ended
on this sacred commute.
Slowly burning the oil,
and flames of my youth.

But I found my way out.
Found a new call from the Divine —
Forever covering you,
with a warning sign.

THE ADDITION OF YEARS

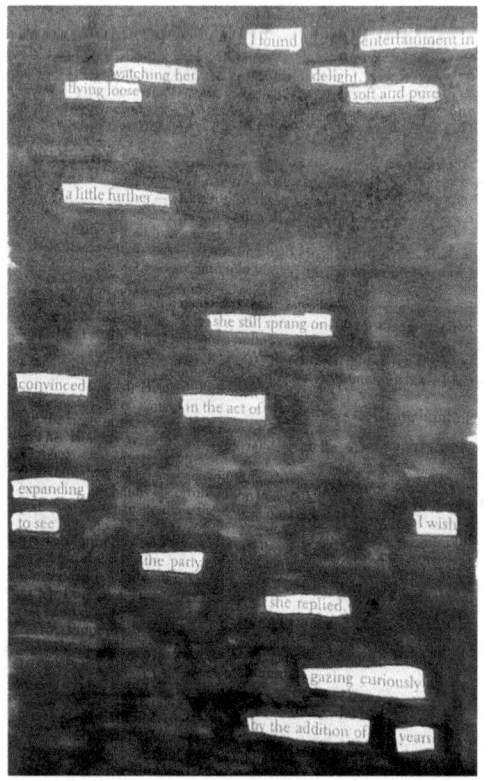

I found entertainment
in watching her delight flying loose.
Soft, and pure.
A little further she still sprang on.
Convinced in the act of expanding.
I wish to see the party, she replied.
Gazing curiously,
by the addition of years.

THE DETAILS

The devils in the details,
they flippantly declare.
Its traces of darkness
embedded like snares.

But I've seen God in the vapors —
Fleeting moments of low fanfair.
Enshrining the finite
with infinite care.

So keep all your demons
and violent affairs,
away from the shrines,
of my
elemental prayers.

VIPER KING

Viper king of twisted schemes,
we came to you for light.
Your devilish snares, keeping us there.
Enslaved by your delight.

But now with swords in hand,
we no longer fear your height.
Emboldened by the truth,
we fight for what is right.

FIXED IT FOR YOU

Amen let's ~~stand.~~
Rest.
Laugh.
Sleep.
Play.
Love.
Breathe.

EXIT MEETING

It's okay to let go.
It's okay to walk away.
You won't stumble
or miss it,
despite what they say.

This welcomed departure,
holds a Presence that stays.
Walking beside you,
to rekindle love's flame.

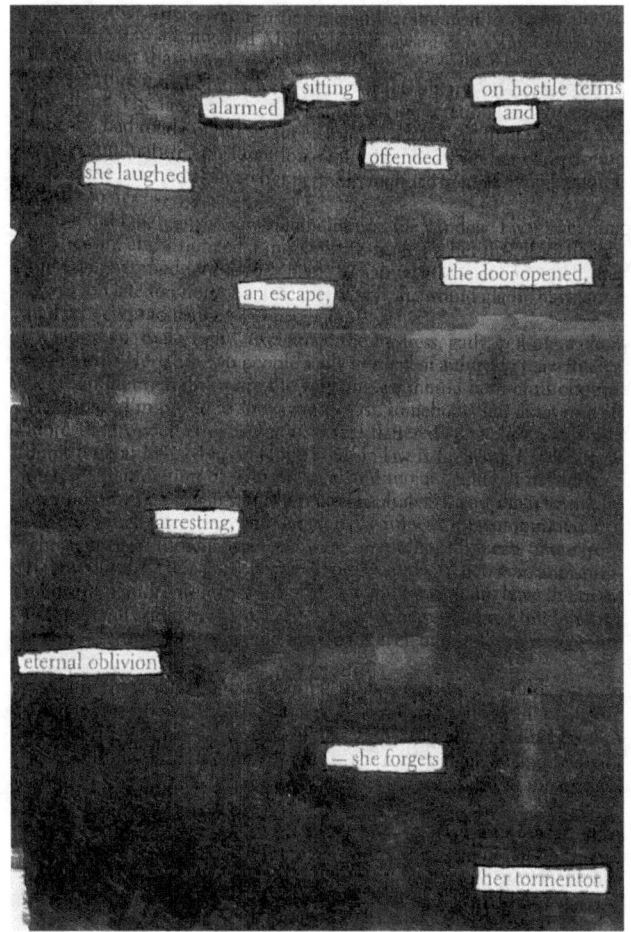

Sitting on hostile terms,
alarmed and offended,
she laughed.
The door opened.
An escape arresting
eternal oblivion —
She forgets her tormentor.

SURVIVING WONDERLAND

My eyelids slowly open,
with a wearied, tired haze. Adjusting to
the stillness
of my
harrowing
escape.

Beside me lay the fragments,
of the watch that once bound me —
Broken upon the impact.
Daily torment now
relieved.

I'm safe from all the ticking.
That endless drone that stole my years.
Time can be rewritten, and
purged of all my fears.

Closing the door to Wonderland,
the weight lifts off my chest.
Seeing wonder that's already here,

in this place of promised rest.

Resources

BOOKS

- *The Road Away from God: How Love Finds Us Even As We Walk Away* by Jonathan Martin
- *Holy Hurt: Understanding Spiritual Trauma and the Process of Healing* by Hillary L. McBride Ph.D.
- *No Bad Parts: Healing Trauma and Restoring Wholeness with the Internal Family Systems Model* by Richard Schwartz Ph.D.
- *Invisible Jesus: A Book about Leaving the Church and Looking for Christ* by Scot McKnight and Tommy Preson Phillips
- *Dinner for Vampires* by Bethany Joy Lenz
- *Do I Stay Christian?* By Brian McCLaren

PODCASTS

- *High Control* hosted by Ally Heny and Scot Lloyd
- *Heaven Bent* hosted by Tara Jeans Stevens
- *Feet of Clay — Confessions of the Cult Sisters* hosted by Sharon Madere and Tracey Phalen
- *You Have Permission* hosted by Dan Koch

Acknowledgments

One thing I've learned through dealing with trauma is that so much of our emotional healing takes place in relationship with other people. I find that especially beautiful, given how often relationships are the source of our deepest pain. With this in mind, there are a few folks I'd love to extend my thanks to.

To Denver Community Church and Highlands Church Denver. I'm deeply grateful to your investment and belief in this project.

To Michelle Wahila, for introducing me to Tehom Center Publishing. I can't thank you enough for reaching out on behalf of a stranger and answering all my questions.

To Dr. Angela Yarber, Bethany Meier-Evans, and the entire Tehom Center Publishing team. I'm so grateful for the opportunity to work with you all. Publishing a book always felt daunting to me, but you greatly eased that burden and gave me a vision for something attainable.

To my IHOPKC recovery groups. Oof, y'all. We have been *through* it. Thank you for your advocacy, and the open space you created so others can feel validated. I hate that we had to go through what we did, but it's an honor to walk through to the other side with you all.

To the former leaders at IHOPKC who bravely brought the allegations of sexual assault forward. Thank you for putting yourselves in the crosshairs for the sake of truth, humility, and justice.

To Deborah Perkins, and all other IHOPKC survivors who've shared their stories of abuse. I am forever in awe of your courage, resilience, and faith. This book would not exist without the light you cracked open. Thank you.

To Aubrey Dixon. This book would also not exist without you. I am forever grateful that our paths aligned just weeks before everything with IHOPKC came out. I was already in such a fragile place, I can't imagine how I would have faired without having you as my counselor. I can't thank you enough for your gentle leadership during that season of my life.

To my Writing Group Gals who read so many more drafts than I intended to send. Your notes, encouragements, and perspectives have elevated this book to a height it couldn't have reached otherwise. Thank you for generously giving your time and talents to hold space for my story and shape it into the best version of itself.

To Joe Santini for being such a joyful light of encouragement as I began my writing journey. The way you made a seemingly overwhelming task feel actionable was an incredible gift to me. Thank you for all your ideas, brainstorming prompts, and Swiftie shorthand notes.

To my Gal Pals and closest friends. I know deep in my bones that I would not be the reclaimed woman I am today without you. You've allowed me to access parts of myself that I didn't know were buried. Thank you for all your love and support.

To my family who has loved me throughout every stage of my spiritual journey. Years ago, some of you asked the hard questions that I believe led to the revelations of this book today.

To my best fren Maggie who is always there to give me comfort, laughter, and endless hugs. You literally held me during some of the hardest moments of processing this book. Thank you for always reminding me about God's goodness.

To my husband Peter for all the tangible and intangible ways you carried me through this writing season. Thank you for cooking meals, watching our pup, listening to me process, and offering a kind perspective when I needed it most.

To my mom who always knew. Ma, thank you for your discernment and voice that has never stopped looking out for me. Your steadfast love, protection, and support will always be an anchor in my life.

Lastly, to every reader who picked up this book. Whether you've experienced spiritual trauma yourself or not, I treasure you dearly and pray you'd feel deeply held by Love.

www.ingramcontent.com/pod-product-compliance
Lightning Source LLC
Chambersburg PA
CBHW061804120626
46550CB00005B/2124